Sit & Learn: Advent Calendar 2024 Entertaining Facts for Every Flush!

Get ready to unwrap a new surprise every day
with this fun-filled advent
Each day reveals a unique (
with mind-boggling facts, (
unexpected discoveries. Fro

CW01500862

science and mysteries of space to bizarre
inventions, odd historical moments, and the
marvels of the natural world, this book will keep
you entertained and curious from December
1st all the way to Christmas Eve.

Whether you're here to learn something new,
impress your friends, or simply make your
bathroom break more interesting, you're in for
a treat! With each flip of the page, you'll dive
deeper into a world of jaw-dropping records,
strange coincidences, and unbelievable truths
that might just change how you see the world.
Plus, for added fun, you'll find trivia challenges
sprinkled throughout to test your knowledge
and keep you on your toes.

Enjoy this holiday adventure, and remember—
learning can be fun, surprising, and perfect for
every flush!

Sit & Learn
ENTERTAINING FACTS FOR EVERY FLUSH
Index:

1. Strange Science
2. History's Mysteries
3. Mind-Blowing Space Facts
4. Animal Kingdom Wonders
5. Cultural Curiosities
6. Technological Marvels
7. Bizarre Human Body Facts
8. Ocean's Deep Secrets
9. Unbelievable Sports Records
10. Food Fun Facts
11. Trivia Challenge
12. World Changers
13. Weird but True: Strange Facts
14. Wacky World Records
15. Crazy Coincidences: Life's Funny Twists
16. Laws That Make You Laugh: Odd Laws
17. Animal Antics: Funny Animal Facts
18. Bizarre Inventions: Unusual Creations
19. Laugh-Out-Loud History
20. Funny Fails: Science Gone Wrong
21. Silly Superstitions: Absurd Beliefs
22. Nature's Extreme Moments
23. Tricky Trivia: Test Your Knowledge!
24. Christmas Curiosities

Day 1: Strange Science

Science is full of surprises and mysteries that can seem almost impossible to believe. Here are some mind-blowing facts from the world of science that are sure to spark your curiosity:

Tsunamis caused by earthquakes can travel as fast as a jet plane

The massive waves generated by underwater earthquakes can reach speeds of over 500 miles per hour, racing across the ocean at an astonishing pace.

Trees "talk" to each other through their roots

Trees in forests use an underground network of fungi to exchange information about threats, such as insect attacks, and even share resources with other trees.

Earth isn't a perfect sphere

While we usually think of our planet as a smooth, round ball, Earth is actually slightly flattened at the poles due to its rotation.

Human bones are lighter
than steel but five times stronger
The bones in our bodies are incredibly strong despite being much lighter than metal. This perfect balance of weight and strength allows us to move efficiently and safely.

In some places in the world, it rains... animals!
Although it sounds like fiction, there have been cases where small creatures, like frogs or fish, were "rained" down during storms. This is explained by strong air currents lifting the animals into the clouds.

Ice can be hot
Under extreme conditions, like those found on some planets, there are forms of ice that are so compressed they reach temperatures of hundreds of degrees, yet they are still technically ice.

Light can be "slowed down"
While light travels at an incredible speed (about 186,282 miles per second in a vacuum), scientists have managed to slow it down to just 17 meters per second by passing it through special materials.

Your body emits light
The human body produces a faint bioluminescent glow, though it's not visible to the naked eye. This light is a result of chemical reactions happening in our cells.

Lightning can strike the same place more than once
Contrary to the popular myth, lightning can and does strike the same spot multiple times. For example, the Eiffel Tower in Paris is hit by lightning regularly.

There's a giant cloud of alcohol in space
Scientists have discovered a massive cloud of ethyl alcohol in space, large enough to fill trillions of bottles. Unfortunately, it's too far away to be of any practical use.

The world of science is full of astonishing facts that show just how diverse and mysterious our universe really is.

Day 2: History's Mysteries

History is filled with strange events, puzzling figures, and unexplained phenomena that continue to baffle us. Here are some of the most intriguing mysteries from the past:

The Lost City of Atlantis

The legend of Atlantis, a powerful and advanced civilization that supposedly sank into the sea, has fascinated people for centuries. Despite many theories, no concrete evidence of its existence has ever been found.

The Voynich Manuscript

This ancient book, filled with mysterious illustrations and written in an unknown language, has puzzled scholars since its discovery in the 15th century. Despite extensive research, the text remains undeciphered to this day.

The Disappearance of the Roanoke Colony

In 1587, a group of English settlers mysteriously vanished from Roanoke Island, leaving behind only the word "CROATOAN" carved into a tree. The fate of the colony remains one of the oldest unsolved mysteries in American history.

The Identity of Jack the Ripper

Jack the Ripper terrorized the streets of London in 1888, killing at least five women. Despite numerous investigations and countless theories, the true identity of the killer was never discovered.

The Mystery of Stonehenge

Built over 5,000 years ago, the massive stones of Stonehenge continue to puzzle archaeologists. How and why these massive stones were transported and arranged remains a mystery, though many theories abound.

The Dancing Plague of 1518

In Strasbourg, France, a strange outbreak occurred where hundreds of people started dancing uncontrollably for days, some even dancing themselves to death. To this day, historians aren't sure what caused this bizarre event.

The Curse of King Tut's Tomb

When the tomb of the Egyptian pharaoh Tutankhamun was discovered in 1922, rumors of a curse spread after several people involved in the excavation died under mysterious circumstances. While some dismiss the curse as superstition, it remains a compelling part of the tomb's legend.

The Bermuda Triangle
This region in the North Atlantic Ocean has long been associated with the mysterious disappearance of ships and planes. Though scientific explanations like extreme weather and human error are common, some believe there is something more mysterious at play.

The Mary Celeste
In 1872, the merchant ship Mary Celeste was found adrift in the Atlantic Ocean, completely intact but with no sign of its crew. What happened to the people on board remains one of maritime history's greatest mysteries.

The Library of Alexandria
Once the largest library in the ancient world, the Library of Alexandria was a center of knowledge and culture. Its destruction, whether by fire or other means, led to the loss of countless works of literature and science. The exact cause and timeline of its fall are still debated.

History holds countless secrets that continue to intrigue and perplex historians and researchers. These enduring mysteries remind us of how much we still have to learn about the past.

Day 3: Mind-Blowing Space Facts

Space is full of mysteries and mind-boggling phenomena that go beyond our everyday experiences. Here are some fascinating space facts that will blow your mind:

A day on Venus is longer than a year
Venus rotates so slowly on its axis that one day on the planet lasts longer than its year. A single day on Venus is about 243 Earth days, while its year is roughly 225 Earth days.

Space is completely silent
In the vacuum of space, there is no atmosphere or air molecules to carry sound waves, making it one of the quietest places in the universe.

There are more stars in the universe than grains of sand on Earth
It's estimated that the observable universe contains about 1 septillion (1 followed by 24 zeros) stars—far more than all the grains of sand on Earth's beaches.

Black holes can spaghettify objects

The gravity of a black hole is so strong that anything coming too close gets stretched into a long, thin shape—a process scientists call "spaghettification."

The universe is expanding

Edwin Hubble discovered that galaxies are moving away from each other, which means the universe is expanding. The farther a galaxy is, the faster it recedes.

It rains diamonds on Jupiter and Saturn

Scientists believe that the intense storms on Jupiter and Saturn may turn methane into diamonds, which then fall as "diamond rain" deep into the planets' atmospheres.

A teaspoon of neutron star matter weighs billions of tons

Neutron stars are some of the densest objects in the universe. The material from one would be so dense that a teaspoon of it could weigh billions of tons.

Jupiter's Great Red Spot is the biggest storm in the universe

This massive storm on Jupiter is larger than the entire Earth and has been raging for at least 300 years.

The Sun makes up over 99% of the mass of the solar system

Although the solar system contains planets, moons, asteroids, and comets, the Sun accounts for 99.86% of its total mass.

Space smells... like burnt steak

Astronauts returning from spacewalks often describe the scent of space as something similar to burnt steak or hot metal. This smell is the result of chemical reactions when space particles interact with spacesuit materials.

Space is not only fascinating but also full of extraordinary phenomena that remind us how little we truly understand about the universe's mysteries.

Day 4: Animal Kingdom Wonders

The animal kingdom is full of astonishing creatures and behaviors that sometimes seem too incredible to be true. Here are some of the most amazing and bizarre facts about animals:

Octopuses have three hearts and blue blood

An octopus has two hearts that pump blood to its gills, and one that pumps blood to the rest of its body. Their blood is blue because it contains copper-based hemocyanin instead of the iron-based hemoglobin that we have.

Cows have best friends

Studies have shown that cows form close bonds with other cows and can become stressed if they are separated from their best friends.

Butterflies taste with their feet

Instead of using a tongue or mouth, butterflies have taste sensors on their feet, allowing them to "taste" food just by standing on it.

Sloths only poop once a week

Sloths are known for their slow lifestyle, and this extends to their digestive systems. They only leave the trees once a week to go to the bathroom.

A group of flamingos is called a "flamboyance"

Flamingos are known for their bright pink color and dramatic social displays, so it's fitting that a group of them is referred to as a "flamboyance."

Male seahorses give birth

In a reversal of traditional reproductive roles, it's the male seahorse that carries the babies and gives birth to them, sometimes hundreds at a time.

A cockroach can live for a week without its head

Cockroaches are incredibly resilient creatures. They can survive for up to a week without a head because their body is able to function without a brain for a short time.

Dolphins have names for each other

Dolphins use unique whistles to call each other, almost like names. They can recognize these calls even after many years apart.

Axolotls can regenerate their limbs

These remarkable amphibians have the ability to regrow entire limbs, organs, and even parts of their spinal cords if injured.

Penguins propose to their mates with pebbles

Male penguins present female penguins with a pebble as a way of proposing. If the female accepts, they will use the pebble to build their nest together.

The animal kingdom is full of wonders that highlight the diversity and complexity of life on Earth. From creatures with unique abilities to fascinating behaviors, the natural world never ceases to amaze.

Day 5: Cultural Curiosities

Every culture has its own unique customs and traditions that can seem unusual or fascinating to outsiders. Here are some intriguing cultural practices from around the world:

Baby jumping in Spain
In the Spanish village of Castrillo de Murcia, an annual festival called "El Colacho" involves men dressed as devils jumping over babies lying on mattresses. This centuries-old tradition is believed to cleanse the babies of original sin and bring good luck.

Throwing furniture out of the window in South Africa
On New Year's Eve, people in some neighborhoods of Johannesburg celebrate by throwing old furniture out of their windows to symbolize getting rid of the old and welcoming the new.

Giraffe women of Myanmar
In the Kayan tribe of Myanmar, women wear brass neck rings from a young age to elongate their necks. These "giraffe women" view the rings as a symbol of beauty and cultural identity.

Turning the dead into beads in South Korea

In South Korea, where space for traditional burials is limited, some families choose to have their loved one's ashes turned into decorative beads, which are then displayed in homes as a way to honor the deceased.

Lip plates in Ethiopia

Among the Mursi tribe of Ethiopia, women wear large clay or wooden plates in their lower lips. The size of the plate is often seen as a symbol of social status or readiness for marriage.

Kanamara Matsuri – Japan's fertility festival

This annual festival in Kawasaki, Japan, celebrates fertility and sexual health. It is best known for its parades featuring giant phallic symbols, which are meant to bring good luck and prosperity.

Polterabend in Germany

Before a wedding in Germany, friends and family of the couple gather to break porcelain plates and other items, as the sound of shattering is believed to bring good fortune to the marriage.

Feeding the dead in Madagascar

In Madagascar, the "Famadihana" ceremony involves exhuming the bodies of deceased relatives, rewrapping them in fresh cloth, and dancing with them in a celebration of life and remembrance.

Foot binding in ancient China

Although now banned, foot binding was a centuries-old practice in China where young girls had their feet tightly bound to keep them small, as tiny feet were considered a symbol of beauty and status.

La Tomatina in Spain

Every year, the town of Buñol in Spain hosts "La Tomatina," a giant tomato fight where thousands of people throw tomatoes at each other in a playful and messy celebration.

Cultures around the world are full of unique traditions that offer insight into their history, values, and beliefs. These cultural curiosities remind us of the incredible diversity of human expression.

Day 6: Technological Marvels

Throughout history, human ingenuity has led to incredible technological advancements that have changed the world. Here are some mind-blowing technological achievements that continue to inspire and amaze:

The Internet

Originally developed in the 1960s as a military communication tool, the internet has since evolved into a global network connecting billions of people, revolutionizing how we communicate, work, and access information.

The Great Wall of China is visible from space

Despite the popular myth, astronauts have confirmed that the Great Wall of China is not easily visible from space with the naked eye. However, with the aid of telescopes, it can be spotted under the right conditions.

The Large Hadron Collider

The world's largest and most powerful particle accelerator, located in Switzerland, can simulate conditions similar to those just after the Big Bang. It has led to groundbreaking discoveries in particle physics, including the Higgs boson.

Smartphones are more powerful than NASA's computers from the 1960s

The average modern smartphone is millions of times more powerful than the computers NASA used to send astronauts to the moon during the Apollo missions.

3D Printing

What started as a novelty is now a transformative technology. 3D printing can create everything from simple toys to complex human organs, and it's being used in industries from medicine to aerospace.

The International Space Station (ISS)

A joint effort between several countries, the ISS is the largest human-made structure in space. It orbits Earth at a speed of about 17,500 miles per hour and serves as a hub for scientific research.

Self-driving cars

Autonomous vehicles, once considered science fiction, are now a reality. Companies around the world are developing self-driving cars that use artificial intelligence and sensors to navigate roads without human input.

CRISPR gene editing
This revolutionary technology allows scientists to edit DNA with remarkable precision. It holds the potential to cure genetic diseases, improve crops, and even alter the traits of future generations.

Robots on Mars
NASA's rovers, such as Curiosity and Perseverance, have been exploring Mars for years, gathering valuable data and searching for signs of ancient life. These robots are some of the most advanced machines ever sent to another planet.

Artificial Intelligence (AI)
AI is becoming a central part of modern technology, from voice-activated assistants like Siri and Alexa to complex algorithms that drive decision-making in industries ranging from healthcare to finance.

Technology continues to push the boundaries of what's possible, and these marvels show just how far human innovation has come. From space exploration to breakthroughs in medicine, the world of technology never ceases to amaze.

Day 7: Bizarre Human Body Facts

The human body is an extraordinary machine, capable of remarkable feats and strange phenomena. Here are some weird and wonderful facts about our bodies that will leave you in awe:

Your stomach gets a new lining every few days

The acids in your stomach are so strong that they could digest your stomach itself. To prevent this, your body replaces the lining of your stomach every three to four days.

You shed millions of skin cells daily

The average person sheds about 30,000 to 40,000 skin cells every minute. Over the course of a year, that adds up to nearly 9 pounds (4 kilograms) of dead skin.

Your bones are constantly regenerating

Every 10 years or so, your skeleton completely regenerates itself. This process helps keep your bones strong, but it also means that technically, you get a "new" skeleton every decade!

The human body contains about 37 trillion cells

Your body is made up of an astonishing 37 trillion cells, each working together to keep you alive and functioning.

Your brain uses more energy than any other organ

Although the brain makes up only about 2% of your body weight, it consumes roughly 20% of your body's energy, making it the most energy-demanding organ.

You're taller in the morning than in the evening

Throughout the day, the discs in your spine get compressed due to gravity, causing you to lose a small amount of height by the evening. When you sleep, your spine decompresses, and you regain that height by morning.

Your heart could power a small device

The human heart generates enough electricity in a day to power a small light bulb. The electrical impulses it produces keep your heart beating and your blood circulating.

The length of all your blood vessels could circle the Earth

If you were to lay out all the blood vessels in your body end to end, they would stretch for about 60,000 miles—enough to circle the Earth more than twice.

The Only Being That Blushes: A Uniquely Human Trait

Blushing is a unique human trait. It's an automatic response triggered by emotions such as embarrassment, making it one of the most mysterious and distinctively human behaviors.

Your body can glow in the dark—just not enough to see it

Human bodies emit a faint bioluminescent light, but it's about 1,000 times weaker than the light our eyes can detect, so we can't see it without special equipment.

The human body is full of strange and fascinating quirks that highlight just how complex and amazing we are. From constant regeneration to our unique ability to blush, these facts remind us of the wonders of being human.

Day 8: Ocean's Deep Secrets

The ocean covers more than 70% of our planet, yet much of it remains unexplored. Below the surface lies a world full of extraordinary creatures and mysterious phenomena. Here are some fascinating facts about the ocean's hidden wonders:

We know more about the moon than our own oceans

Despite covering most of the Earth, less than 20% of the ocean has been explored. In contrast, we have mapped almost 100% of the moon's surface.

The deepest part of the ocean is deeper than Mount Everest is tall

The Mariana Trench in the Pacific Ocean is the deepest point on Earth, plunging nearly 36,000 feet (about 11,000 meters) below sea level— deeper than the height of Mount Everest, which stands at about 29,000 feet.

The ocean produces over half of the world's oxygen

Tiny marine plants called phytoplankton produce at least 50% of the Earth's oxygen, making the ocean a crucial part of the planet's life-support system.

More people have been to space than the bottom of the ocean

Fewer than 10 people have ever ventured to the bottom of the Mariana Trench, while over 500 astronauts have been to space. The extreme pressure at these depths makes exploration incredibly difficult.

There are underwater rivers and lakes

Some parts of the ocean floor have pockets of highly salty water that are so dense they form "underwater rivers" or "lakes." These brine pools create a stunning contrast from the surrounding water and are often toxic to marine life.

The largest waterfall on Earth is underwater

The Denmark Strait cataract, located between Greenland and Iceland, is the world's largest waterfall. It plunges about 11,500 feet—more than three times the height of Angel Falls, the tallest waterfall on land.

The ocean contains more historical artifacts than all the world's museums combined

It's estimated that over 3 million shipwrecks are scattered across the ocean floor, along with countless other lost treasures and artifacts from centuries of seafaring history.

Giant squids are real

For centuries, sailors spoke of sea monsters called krakens. These tales turned out to be based on real creatures: giant squids, which can grow up to 43 feet long and live in the deep ocean.

There's more gold in the ocean than you think

The ocean holds an estimated 20 million tons of gold, dissolved in seawater. However, extracting it is currently too expensive to be practical.

The ocean glows in the dark

Bioluminescent organisms, like plankton and jellyfish, can produce their own light. These glowing creatures create breathtaking displays, lighting up the ocean with eerie, otherworldly beauty.

The ocean's depths are home to countless secrets and wonders, many of which we have yet to discover. From mysterious creatures to natural phenomena, the hidden world beneath the waves is a source of endless fascination.

Day 9: Unbelievable Sports Records

The world of sports is filled with incredible achievements that defy expectations and push the limits of human potential. Here are some of the most unbelievable sports records that continue to amaze fans around the globe:

The Longest Tennis Match

In 2010, John Isner and Nicolas Mahut played the longest tennis match in history at Wimbledon. The match lasted 11 hours and 5 minutes over the course of three days, with Isner finally winning 70-68 in the fifth set.

Most Olympic Gold Medals

American swimmer Michael Phelps holds the record for the most Olympic gold medals, having won 23 golds throughout his career. His total of 28 Olympic medals makes him the most decorated Olympian of all time.

Fastest 100m Sprint

Usain Bolt set the world record for the fastest 100-meter sprint in 2009, clocking in at 9.58 seconds. His incredible speed earned him the title of the fastest man alive.

Youngest Professional Soccer Player

Mauricio Baldivieso from Bolivia became the youngest professional soccer player ever when he debuted at the age of 12 years and 362 days for Club Aurora in 2009.

Most Consecutive NBA Championships

The Boston Celtics hold the record for the most consecutive NBA championships, winning eight titles in a row from 1959 to 1966. This incredible dynasty remains unmatched in basketball history.

The Longest Winning Streak in Sports

Jahangir Khan, a Pakistani squash player, holds the record for the longest winning streak in any sport. From 1981 to 1986, he won 555 consecutive matches, a feat that has yet to be surpassed in any competitive sport.

The Highest Scoring Basketball Game

The highest-scoring NBA game took place in 1983 between the Detroit Pistons and the Denver Nuggets, with a total of 370 points scored. The Pistons won the game 186-184 in triple overtime.

Most Points in a Single NHL Season

Wayne Gretzky, known as "The Great One," holds the record for the most points in a single NHL season with 215 points during the 1985-1986 season. His dominance in hockey is legendary, and he holds numerous other records.

The Fastest Marathon Time

Eliud Kipchoge of Kenya made history in 2019 when he became the first person to run a marathon in under two hours. Though his time of 1:59:40 was not an official world record due to specific conditions, it is still regarded as a monumental achievement.

Most Home Runs in a Single MLB Season

Barry Bonds holds the record for the most home runs in a single Major League Baseball season,
· hitting 73 home runs in 2001. His total of 762 career home runs is also the highest in MLB history.

Sports records like these showcase the extraordinary abilities of athletes and serve as reminders of how much the human body can achieve. Whether through sheer determination, talent, or perseverance, these incredible feats continue to inspire athletes and fans alike.

Day 10: Food Fun Facts

Food is a central part of our lives, and the world of food is filled with surprising and fascinating facts. Here are some fun and quirky food-related facts that you might not know:

Honey never spoils

Archaeologists have found pots of honey in ancient Egyptian tombs that are over 3,000 years old—and still perfectly edible! Honey's natural properties make it one of the few foods that doesn't go bad.

Chocolate was once used as currency

The ancient Maya and Aztec civilizations used cacao beans as a form of currency. For them, chocolate was not just a luxury food, but a valuable commodity.

The most expensive pizza in the world costs $12,000

The world's most expensive pizza, called the "Louis XIII," is made in Italy and costs a whopping $12,000. It takes 72 hours to prepare and includes ingredients like three types of caviar, organic buffalo mozzarella, and edible gold.

Carrots were originally purple

The orange carrots we eat today were selectively bred in the Netherlands in the 17th century. Before that, most carrots were purple, yellow, or white.

Bananas are berries, but strawberries are not

In botanical terms, bananas are classified as berries because they develop from a single flower with one ovary. Surprisingly, strawberries do not meet the botanical criteria to be considered true berries.

Pineapples take two years to grow

While they may seem like fast-growing tropical fruits, pineapples take about two years to mature from planting to harvest, which is why they can be expensive.

Peppers don't actually burn your mouth

The sensation of heat from spicy peppers is actually a chemical reaction. Capsaicin, the compound in peppers, tricks your brain into thinking your mouth is on fire, even though there's no actual heat.

The largest watermelon ever grown weighed over 350 pounds

The world's largest watermelon, grown in Tennessee in 2013, tipped the scales at 350.5 pounds (about 159 kilograms). That's heavier than an average adult!

Potatoes were the first food to be grown in space

In 1995, NASA and the University of Wisconsin developed a way to grow potatoes in space aboard the space shuttle Columbia, marking the first time food was successfully cultivated outside of Earth.

A single cup of coffee can contain over 1,000 chemicals

Coffee is one of the most chemically complex drinks we consume, with over 1,000 different compounds contributing to its flavor and aroma. That complexity is part of what makes each cup of coffee unique.

Food is not only a necessity for life but also full of surprising facts and interesting stories that highlight its importance in history, science, and culture. From ancient traditions to modern marvels, the world of food continues to amaze and delight.

Day 11: Trivia Challenge:

Think you can get them all right? Choose your answers from the options provided, and check at the end of each section to see how you did!

1. Science
Q1: What is the only planet in our solar system that rotates on its side?
a) Venus b) Uranus c) Neptune

Q2: How many bones are in the human body?
a) 206 b) 198 c) 222

Q3: What is the hardest natural substance on Earth?
a) Gold b) Quartz c) Diamond

Q4: What element does the chemical symbol 'O' represent?
a) Oxygen b) Osmium c) Ozone

Q5: How long does it take for light from the sun to reach Earth?
a) 1 minute b) 8 minutes c) 30 minutes

2. History

Q1: Who was the first President of the United States?
a) Thomas Jefferson b) George Washington c) John Adams

Q2: What year did the Titanic sink?
a) 1912 b) 1915 c) 1920

Q3: Who was the first woman to fly solo across the Atlantic Ocean?
a) Amelia Earhart b) Harriet Quimby c) Bessie Coleman

Q4: What ancient civilization built the pyramids?
a) Romans b) Mayans c) Egyptians

Q5: Which war was fought between the North and South regions in the United States?
a) Revolutionary War
b) Civil War
c) World War I

3. Geography

Q1: **What is the largest desert in the world?**
a) Sahara Desert
b) Antarctic Desert
c) Arabian Desert

Q2: **Which river is the longest in the world?**
a) Amazon River
b) Mississippi River
c) Nile River

Q3: **What is the capital city of Canada?**
a) Toronto b) Ottawa c) Montreal

Q4: **Mount Everest is located in which two countries?**
a) Nepal and China
b) India and Bhutan
c) Pakistan and India

Q5: **What is the smallest country in the world by land area?**
a) Monaco
b) Vatican City
c) Liechtenstein

4. Pop Culture

Q1: Who is the famous fictional wizard with a lightning bolt scar on his forehead?
a) Harry Potter b) Merlin c) Gandalf

Q2: Which animated film features a talking snowman named Olaf?
a) Toy Story
b) Frozen
c) Tangled

Q3: What band was Beyoncé originally a part of?
a) Spice Girls b) TLC c) Destiny's Child

Q4: Which movie features the quote, "May the Force be with you"?
a) Star Wars
b) The Matrix
c) Lord of the Rings

Q5: Who played the character of Jack in the movie Titanic?
a) Tom Cruise
b) Leonardo DiCaprio
c) Brad Pitt

5. Sports

Q1: How many players are on a basketball team on the court at one time?
a) Five b) Six c) Seven

Q2: What sport is known as "America's pastime"?
a) Football
b) Basketball
c) Baseball

Q3: Who holds the record for the most home runs in Major League Baseball?
a) Babe Ruth
b) Hank Aaron
c) Barry Bonds

Q4: In what year were the first modern Olympic Games held?
a) 1896 b) 1900 c) 1912

Q5: What is the only country to have played in every single soccer World Cup?
a) Germany
b) Argentina
c) Brazil

6. Animals

Q1: **What is the fastest land animal in the world?**
a) Cheetah b) Lion c) Gazelle

Q2: **How many hearts does an octopus have?**
a) One b) Three c) Four

Q3: **Which bird is known for its colorful display and dancing to attract mates?**
a) Flamingo
b) Peacock
c) Parrot

Q4: **What type of animal is a Komodo dragon?**
a) Snake b) Lizard c) Crocodile

Q5: **Which animal is known as the "King of the Jungle"?**
a) Tiger
b) Elephant
c) Lion

Answers

1 Science:
1. b. Uranus
2. a. 206
3. c. Diamond
4. a. Oxygen
5. b. 8 minutes

2 History:
1. b. George Washington
2. a. 1912
3. a. Amelia Earhart
4. c. Egyptians
5. b. Civil War

3 Geography:
1. b. Antarctic Desert
2. c. Nile River
3. b. Ottawa
4. a. Nepal and China
5. b. Vatican City

4 Pop Culture:
1. a. Harry Potter
2. b. Frozen
3. c. Destiny's Child
4. a. Star Wars
5. b. Leonardo DiCaprio

5 Sports:
1. a. Five
2. c. Baseball
3. c. Barry Bonds
4. a. 1896
5. c. Brazil

6 Animals:
1. a. Cheetah
2. b. Three
3. b. Peacock
4. b. Lizard
5. c. Lion

Day 12. World Changers: Famous People Who Changed History

1. Albert Einstein
A physicist who developed the theory of relativity, revolutionizing our understanding of space and time.

2. Marie Curie
A pioneering scientist in radioactivity, the first woman to win a Nobel Prize, and the only person to win in two different scientific fields.

3. Martin Luther King Jr.
A civil rights leader who advocated for racial equality through nonviolent resistance, delivering the iconic "I Have a Dream" speech.

4. Mahatma Gandhi
An Indian activist who used nonviolent civil disobedience to lead India to independence from British rule.

5. Steve Jobs
Co-founder of Apple Inc., who revolutionized personal technology with innovations like the iPhone and iPad.

6. Nelson Mandela

The first black president of South Africa and a global symbol of resistance against apartheid.

7. Leonardo da Vinci

A Renaissance genius known for masterpieces like the Mona Lisa and The Last Supper, as well as his innovative inventions.

8. Rosa Parks

A civil rights activist whose refusal to give up her bus seat became a symbol of the fight against racial segregation.

9. Thomas Edison

Inventor of the electric light bulb and phonograph, among many other things, shaping the modern industrial age.

10. Malala Yousafzai

An advocate for girls' education and the youngest Nobel Prize laureate, who survived a Taliban assassination attempt.

11. Isaac Newton

The father of modern physics, Newton's laws of motion and universal gravitation shaped our understanding of the natural world.

12. Abraham Lincoln

The 16th president of the United States, Lincoln led the country through the Civil War and abolished slavery with the Emancipation Proclamation.

13. Alexander Graham Bell

Inventor of the telephone, Bell revolutionized global communication.

14. Florence Nightingale

The founder of modern nursing, Nightingale improved healthcare and hygiene standards during the Crimean War.

15. William Shakespeare

The greatest playwright in history, Shakespeare's works like Hamlet and Romeo and Juliet have had a lasting impact on literature and theater.

16. Galileo Galilei

An astronomer and physicist, Galileo is known for his support of heliocentrism and his contributions to modern science.

17. Queen Elizabeth I
The Queen of England during the Golden Age, she led the country through a time of cultural flourishing and defeated the Spanish Armada.

18. Vincent van Gogh
A Dutch post-impressionist painter whose works like Starry Night revolutionized modern art.

19. Henry Ford
Founder of Ford Motor Company, Ford revolutionized industrial production with the assembly line, making cars affordable to the masses.

20. Susan B. Anthony
A leader in the women's suffrage movement, Anthony fought for women's rights, particularly the right to vote.

21. Nikola Tesla
An inventor and electrical engineer whose contributions to alternating current (AC) power systems changed modern electricity use.

22. Winston Churchill

The British Prime Minister during World War II, Churchill led the United Kingdom through its darkest hours.

23. Mother Teresa

A Roman Catholic nun who devoted her life to helping the poor and sick in India, winning a Nobel Peace Prize for her humanitarian work.

24. Charles Darwin

The naturalist whose theory of evolution by natural selection changed our understanding of biology.

25. Franklin D. Roosevelt

The U.S. president who led the country through the Great Depression and most of World War II with his New Deal programs.

26. Ludwig van Beethoven

A German composer and pianist whose music remains among the most influential in Western classical music history.

27. Harriet Tubman

An abolitionist who helped lead hundreds of enslaved people to freedom via the Underground Railroad.

28. Pablo Picasso

A Spanish painter and sculptor, Picasso co-founded the Cubist movement and is considered one of the greatest artists of the 20th century.

29. Sigmund Freud

The father of psychoanalysis, Freud's theories on the unconscious mind influenced psychology, culture, and art.

30. Confucius

An ancient Chinese philosopher whose teachings on ethics, morality, and government continue to shape East Asian cultures.

31. Eleanor Roosevelt

A former First Lady of the United States and a leader in the promotion of human rights, especially women's and civil rights.

Day 13: Weird but True:
Strange Facts You Won't Believe

The world is a weird place, full of unexpected and bizarre facts that might make you scratch your head in disbelief. Here are some strange, yet true, facts that will leave you amazed:

Sharks are older than trees
Sharks have been swimming in the oceans for over 400 million years, while the first trees appeared around 350 million years ago. This means sharks are older than trees!

Bananas are radioactive
Bananas contain potassium, and a small fraction of that potassium is a radioactive isotope. But don't worry—it's not harmful in the amounts found in a banana.

Humans share 60% of their DNA with bananas
While it may seem bananas, humans actually share about 60% of their genetic material with this yellow fruit.

There's a town in Norway where it's illegal to die

In the town of Longyearbyen, located in the Arctic Circle, it's illegal to die because the ground is so cold that bodies won't decompose. If you're terminally ill, you have to be sent to the mainland!

You can hear a blue whale's heartbeat from over 2 miles away

The heart of a blue whale can weigh up to 1,300 pounds (about the size of a small car), and its beat is so powerful that it can be heard from miles away underwater.

Sloths can hold their breath longer than dolphins

While dolphins can hold their breath for about 10 minutes, sloths can slow down their metabolism and hold their breath underwater for up to 40 minutes!

There's a species of jellyfish that is biologically immortal

The jellyfish Turritopsis dohrnii has the ability to revert its cells to an earlier stage of life, meaning it can technically live forever under the right conditions.

A single strand of human hair can hold up to 3.5 ounces of weight

Human hair is stronger than you think—just one strand can support up to 100 grams (3.5 ounces), which is about the weight of a chocolate bar.

There's a lake in Australia that's naturally pink

Lake Hillier in Australia is famous for its bright pink color, which is caused by algae and bacteria in the water.
And yes, you can swim in it!

Goats have rectangular pupils

If you ever look into a goat's eyes, you might notice something unusual—their pupils are rectangular! This helps them see in almost panoramic vision, which is useful for spotting predators.

Koalas have fingerprints just like humans

Koalas have fingerprints that are nearly identical to human fingerprints. In fact, even under a microscope, it's difficult to tell the difference between them.

You lose about 30,000 skin cells every minute

Your skin is constantly shedding dead cells, and you lose roughly 30,000 to 40,000 of them every minute. Over a year, that adds up to about 9 pounds of dead skin!

Wombat poop is cube-shaped

Wombats, native to Australia, are known for producing cube-shaped poop. This unique shape helps keep the poop from rolling away, marking their territory more effectively.

There are more trees on Earth than stars in the Milky Way

It's estimated that there are about 3 trillion trees on Earth, while the Milky Way contains between 100 billion and 400 billion stars.

Dolphins have names for each other

Dolphins use specific whistles to identify and call out to each other, almost like how humans use names.

Bees can recognize human faces

Bees may have tiny brains, but they are surprisingly good at recognizing human faces! They can remember facial features and distinguish one person from another.

Day 14: Wacky World Records:
The Funniest and Weirdest Achievements

The Guinness World Records is full of bizarre and hilarious achievements that defy logic and leave us amazed.
Here are some of the funniest and weirdest records from around the globe:

Most T-Shirts Worn at Once

In 2019, Ted Hastings from Canada set the record by wearing 260 T-shirts at the same time. It took hours to layer up, but he managed to squeeze into all of them.

Fastest Time to Eat a Bowl of Pasta

Michelle Lesco, an American competitive eater, holds the record for devouring a bowl of pasta in just 26.69 seconds.
That's some serious carb loading!

Longest Fingernails Ever

Lee Redmond from the USA holds the record for the longest fingernails, which she grew over 30 years to reach a combined length of 28 feet 4 inches (8.65 meters). She stopped cutting them in 1979!

Most Spoons Balanced on the Body

Dalibor Jablanovic from Serbia balanced an incredible 79 spoons on his body at once in 2016. It's a strange talent, but it got him a place in the record books!

Largest Collection of Rubber Ducks

Charlotte Lee from the USA has collected over 9,000 rubber ducks, earning her the title of the largest rubber duck collection in the world.

Most Toothpicks in a Beard

In 2018, Joel Strasser from the USA broke the record by sticking 3,500 toothpicks into his beard. It took over three hours to achieve this prickly feat.

World's Largest Pizza

The world's largest pizza was made in Rome, Italy, in 2012. It covered an area of 13,580 square feet (1,261 square meters) and was named "Ottavia" in honor of the first Roman emperor.

Tallest Mohawk

Kazuhiro Watanabe from Japan holds the record for the world's tallest mohawk, which stands at 3 feet 8.6 inches (1.13 meters). His hair is truly gravity-defying!

Fastest Time to Assemble a Mr. Potato Head

In 2010, Leighton Barber from the UK set the record for assembling a Mr. Potato Head toy in 5.43 seconds. It's all about precision and speed!

Most Big Macs Eaten in a Lifetime

Donald Gorske from the USA has eaten over 32,000 Big Macs since 1972. He eats about two a day and has no plans to stop anytime soon!

Longest Time Spent in Full Body Contact with Ice

Wim Hof, known as "The Iceman," spent 1 hour, 52 minutes, and 42 seconds fully submerged in ice in 2013. His ability to withstand extreme cold is legendary.

Most Straws Stuffed
in a Mouth (Hands-Free)

In 2018, Nataraj Mahal from India broke the record by fitting 459 straws into his mouth without using his hands. How he did it is anyone's guess!

Fastest Time to Run
a Marathon Dressed as a Vegetable

In 2017, Andrew Lawrence from the UK ran the London Marathon dressed as a carrot in just 2 hours, 59 minutes, and 33 seconds, breaking the record for the fastest marathon dressed as a vegetable.

Largest Human Mattress Dominoes

In 2016, 2,016 participants in China set the record for the largest human mattress dominoes, toppling one another on mattresses in perfect coordination.

Most Watermelons Chopped
on the Stomach in One Minute

In 2018, Ashrita Furman from the USA broke his own record by chopping 26 watermelons placed on his assistant's stomach in one minute. Talk about trust!

Day 15: Crazy Coincidences: When Life Gets Funny

Sometimes life has a way of surprising us with coincidences so bizarre, they seem almost unbelievable. Here are some of the funniest and strangest coincidences that will leave you scratching your head:

The Twin Brothers' Identical Lives

In 1940, twin brothers in Ohio, who had been separated at birth and raised by different families, reunited at the age of 39. Both were named James, both had married women named Linda, both had sons named James Allan, and both later divorced and remarried women named Betty. They also both had dogs named Toy. Talk about a case of identical lives!

Edgar Allan Poe's Eerie Prediction

In his book The Narrative of Arthur Gordon Pym of Nantucket (1838), Edgar Allan Poe wrote about a shipwreck where the survivors, stranded at sea, resort to cannibalism and eat a cabin boy named Richard Parker. Forty-six years later, a real-life shipwreck occurred, and the survivors ate a cabin boy—also named Richard Parker.

The Mysterious Falling Babies

In 1937, a baby named Joseph Figlock was saved from a fall when he landed on a man walking below. One year later, the same baby fell from a window and landed on the same man—Joseph Figlock—who saved him once again.

The Bullet That Found Its Way

In 1883, Henry Ziegland broke up with his girlfriend, who tragically took her own life. Her brother, enraged, shot at Ziegland, believing he had killed him. However, the bullet grazed Ziegland's face and lodged in a tree. Years later, Ziegland decided to blow up the tree with dynamite, not knowing the bullet was still inside. The explosion caused the bullet to dislodge and hit Ziegland, killing him.

The Curse of the Pharaohs

In 1922, when King Tutankhamun's tomb was discovered, several people involved in the excavation mysteriously died. However, the strangest coincidence came in 1972 when a museum curator named Dr. Gamal Mehrez oversaw an exhibition of Tutankhamun's treasures. He declared there was no such thing as a curse, and just a few hours later, he died of a heart attack.

Mark Twain's Coincidental Birth and Death

Famous author Mark Twain was born in 1835, the same year Halley's Comet passed by Earth. In 1909, Twain predicted that he would die the next time the comet appeared. Sure enough, Twain passed away in 1910, the day after Halley's Comet returned.

The Kennedy and Lincoln Parallels

The coincidences between Abraham Lincoln and John F. Kennedy are mind-blowing. Both were elected to Congress in '46 (1846 and 1946), both became president in '60 (1860 and 1960), both were assassinated on a Friday, both were succeeded by vice presidents named Johnson, and both assassins were known by their three names: John Wilkes Booth and Lee Harvey Oswald.

The King Who Died Laughing

King Martin of Aragon died in 1410 from uncontrollable laughter. He was suffering from indigestion when his favorite jester, Borra, told him a joke so funny that the king laughed non-stop, leading to his unexpected demise.

The Car That Saved Two Presidents
The same car was used to transport both Archduke Franz Ferdinand in 1914 and Adolf Hitler in the 1930s. Franz Ferdinand's assassination led to World War I, and Hitler's rise led to World War II. The car, known as Gräf & Stift, became infamous for being at the center of two of the most important historical events of the 20th century.

The Mystery of the Double Book
In the 1920s, Anne Parrish, an American novelist, was browsing a Paris bookstore when she came across her favorite childhood book Jack Frost and Other Stories. She showed it to her husband, who opened the book and found it had her name written inside—her own childhood copy of the book had found its way back to her across the ocean.

The Death of King Umberto I
On July 29, 1900, King Umberto I of Italy met a man who looked exactly like him, who also happened to be named Umberto. The man was born on the same day as the king and in the same town. They both married women named Margherita, and the day after they met, both men were shot dead.

Day 16: Laws That Make You Laugh: The Weirdest Laws Around the World

Throughout history, governments have enacted some bizarre laws that leave us wondering, "How did this become a rule?" Whether these laws were created out of necessity or pure oddity, they continue to amuse and bewilder us today. Here are some of the strangest and funniest laws from around the world:

No Chewing Gum in Singapore

In Singapore, it's illegal to chew gum unless it's for medical reasons. The law was introduced in 1992 to keep public spaces clean after officials became fed up with discarded gum causing damage to public property.

You Can't Wear a Suit of Armor in Parliament (United Kingdom)

Since the medieval period, it has been illegal to wear a suit of armor in the British Parliament. The law was meant to prevent knights from starting fights while heavily armed!

It's Illegal to Wake a Sleeping Bear to Take a Photo (Alaska, USA)

In Alaska, waking a bear to take a selfie is against the law. Understandably, it's probably not the safest idea, either!

No High Heels at Ancient Sites (Greece)

In Greece, it's illegal to wear high heels at ancient sites like the Acropolis. The concern is that sharp heels could cause damage to the historical structures.

You Must Walk Your Dog Daily (Rome, Italy)

In Rome, it's required by law to walk your dog at least once a day. Failure to do so can result in a fine. The city takes pet welfare very seriously!

No Frowning in Milan (Italy)

In Milan, it is legally required to smile at all times, except during funerals or hospital visits. The law, dating back to the 19th century, was intended to promote cheerfulness among citizens.

No Fish in the City Limits (Seattle, USA)

It's illegal to carry fish across the city limits of Seattle without it being safely packed. This law was introduced to maintain cleanliness and prevent fishy smells in the city.

No Chicken Crossings Allowed (Quitman, Georgia, USA)

In the small town of Quitman, Georgia, it's illegal for chickens to cross the road. This law, while probably never enforced, was created to keep poultry contained within the owner's property.

Don't Feed the Pigeons (Venice, Italy)

Feeding pigeons in Venice's St. Mark's Square is illegal. Authorities implemented this law to protect the city's historic monuments from damage caused by pigeon droppings.

No Flushing Toilets After 10 PM (Switzerland)

In Switzerland, it is illegal to flush a toilet after 10 PM in apartment buildings. The law is intended to reduce noise disturbances for neighbors in shared buildings.

Watch What You Name Your Pig (France)

In France, it's illegal to name your pig "Napoleon." The law is a sign of respect for the country's famous military leader and emperor.

No Blue Jeans in North Korea

In North Korea, it's illegal to wear blue jeans because they are considered a symbol of American imperialism. The country has strict regulations regarding what clothing is allowed.

Don't Wear Lacy Underwear (Russia)

In Russia, it's illegal to wear lacy underwear. The law was passed for health and hygiene reasons, though it's one of the stranger fashion regulations around.

Don't Stop Your Car for Pedestrians (Beijing, China)

It's actually illegal to stop your car for pedestrians in Beijing. This bizarre law is meant to keep traffic moving and avoid accidents, though it seems quite risky for pedestrians!

Day 17: Animal Antics: Funniest Facts from the Animal Kingdom

The animal kingdom is full of fascinating creatures with unique behaviors that often leave us laughing in amazement. From clever tricks to outright absurdities, here are some of the funniest facts about animals that will surely bring a smile to your face:

Cows Have Best Friends
Believe it or not, cows form strong social bonds with certain other cows and become stressed when they are separated from their best friends. They are much more social than you might think!

Penguins Propose with Pebbles
Male penguins often present a pebble to the female penguin as a sign of affection and a proposal for nesting. If she accepts, they use the pebble to build their nest together—penguin romance at its finest!

Squirrels Forget Where They Bury Their Nuts

Squirrels are known for burying nuts for later use, but studies show that they forget where they've hidden up to 74% of them. Those forgotten nuts often sprout into new trees!

Otters Hold Hands When They Sleep

Sea otters hold hands while floating in the water to keep from drifting apart while they sleep. This adorable habit ensures they stay close to one another and don't get lost in the current.

Pigeons Can Do Math

Pigeons have been shown to understand basic math and can even recognize the difference between sequences of numbers. Maybe that's why they always know how to find their way home!

A Group of Flamingos is Called a "Flamboyance"

When flamingos gather together in large groups, they are called a "flamboyance," which is a fitting name given their bright pink feathers and elegant posture.

Sloths Are So Slow
That Algae Grows on Them
Sloths move so slowly that algae grow on their fur, giving them a greenish tint that helps them blend in with their surroundings.

Dolphins Give Each Other Names
Dolphins have signature whistles that they use to identify each other, essentially giving themselves names. They use these unique sounds to call out to specific members of their pod.

Kangaroos Can't Walk Backwards
Due to the unique structure of their legs and tail, kangaroos are physically unable to walk backwards. They can only move forward— always hopping ahead in life!

The Heart of a Shrimp
is Located in Its Head
Shrimp have their hearts located in their heads, making them truly headstrong creatures!

Elephants Are Afraid of Bees

Despite their massive size, elephants are terrified of bees. Farmers in some parts of Africa even use beehives to keep elephants away from their crops.

Turtles Can Breathe Through Their Butts

Some species of turtles, like the Australian Fitzroy River turtle, can absorb oxygen through their rear ends, which allows them to stay underwater for extended periods of time.

Horses Can't Vomit

Unlike most animals, horses are unable to vomit due to the strength of the valve between their stomach and esophagus. This unique trait can sometimes lead to serious digestive issues.

Octopuses Have Three Hearts and Blue Blood

Octopuses have three hearts—two pump blood to their gills, while one pumps it to the rest of the body. Their blood is also blue because it contains copper-based hemocyanin, which is better for transporting oxygen in cold, low-oxygen environments.

Day 18: Bizarre Inventions: The Most Unusual Creations Ever Made

Throughout history, inventors have come up with some truly bizarre creations that leave us wondering, "What were they thinking?" While some of these inventions may seem strange or unnecessary, they showcase human creativity and the desire to solve unusual problems. Here are some of the most unusual and hilarious inventions ever made:

The Facekini

Popularized in China, the facekini is a full-face mask designed to protect wearers from the sun while at the beach. It covers the entire face, leaving holes for the eyes, nose, and mouth. While it looks more like a mask for a superhero or villain, it serves a practical purpose for sun protection.

The Banana Slicer

Tired of slicing bananas the old-fashioned way with a knife? The banana slicer offers an oddly specific solution to cut your bananas into even slices in seconds. It's strange but surprisingly popular!

The Pet Rock
In the 1970s, Gary Dahl came up with the idea of selling ordinary rocks as "pets." He marketed them as low-maintenance companions, complete with a cardboard box and breathing holes. As bizarre as it sounds, millions of pet rocks were sold.

The Ostrich Pillow
Designed for napping on the go, the ostrich pillow is a soft, padded head covering that envelops your entire head, providing a cozy cocoon for spontaneous naps. Its odd design makes it look like something out of a sci-fi movie, but it's surprisingly comfortable!

The Dogbrella
For the dog owner who wants to keep their pooch dry in the rain, the dogbrella is a small umbrella that attaches to your dog's leash, keeping them protected from getting soaked while out on a walk.

The Fish Walker

If you've ever felt the urge to take your fish for a walk, the fish walker is for you. This invention consists of a mobile fish tank with wheels and a handle, allowing you to take your goldfish for a stroll around town. While it's more of a novelty item, it definitely turns heads!

The Diet Water

Yes, you read that right—diet water! This product, marketed in Japan, claimed to be a healthier alternative to regular water. Though it's hard to imagine how water could be more "diet," the concept still managed to attract attention.

The Butter Stick

The butter stick is essentially a glue stick but filled with butter instead of glue. It was designed to make spreading butter on toast or other foods easier and less messy. While it's a bit odd, it certainly has its fans!

The Selfie Toaster
Why settle for regular toast when you can have your face on it? The selfie toaster allows you to customize your toast with an image of your face (or someone else's) by burning the pattern onto the bread. It's a strange way to start your day, but undeniably fun!

The Baby Mop
Why clean the floor yourself when your baby can do it? The baby mop is a onesie outfitted with mop-like pads on the arms and legs, allowing your little one to "clean" the floor as they crawl around. Practical or just plain weird?

The Toilet Paper Hat
This wearable roll of toilet paper is meant to keep tissues on hand whenever you need them. The roll sits on top of your head, making it easily accessible for a runny nose or a spill. It's one of the more bizarre headgear designs you'll ever see!

The Sleeping Bag with Arms and Legs

Traditional sleeping bags can feel restrictive, so someone invented the sleeping bag with arms and legs for ultimate mobility and comfort. You can walk, stretch, and even dance while staying cozy inside your sleeping bag.

The Cat Duster Slippers

Love cats and hate dusting? These slippers come with microfiber dusters on the bottom so your cat can clean the floor while wandering around the house. It's a fun, if not slightly strange, way to combine feline companionship with housekeeping.

The Goldfish Walker

Similar to the fish walker, but more portable, this invention is a small, handheld fishbowl designed to take your goldfish out for a day trip. While fish may not enjoy the adventure, it certainly gives their owners something to talk about!

The Hamster Shredder

This is an office paper shredder that also doubles as a hamster wheel. As the hamster runs on the wheel, the shredder destroys unwanted papers. It's a creative way to combine pet care with office work, though we're not sure how much paper shredding the hamster really enjoys.

The Car Exhaust Grill

This bizarre invention allows you to cook food on your car's exhaust system while driving. It's essentially a metal grill that attaches to the exhaust pipe, so you can grill a burger or a steak on the go. The question is, would you want to eat it?

The Baby Stroller and Scooter Combo

For active parents, this strange combo combines a baby stroller with a scooter. Parents can push their baby while riding a scooter, making for an oddly entertaining, albeit slightly dangerous, mode of transportation.

Day 19: Laugh-Out-Loud History: Hilarious Moments from the Past

History is often remembered for its battles, revolutions, and inventions, but it's also full of hilarious and bizarre moments that remind us that people in the past had their share of oddball humor and unexpected situations. Here are some of the funniest moments from history that will leave you laughing out loud:

Peter the Great's Beard Tax

In 1698, Russian Tsar Peter the Great decided that beards were unfashionable and imposed a tax on anyone who wanted to keep their facial hair. Men had to carry around a "beard token" to prove they had paid the tax, and failure to do so meant their beard could be forcibly shaved.

Caligula Declared War on Neptune

The infamous Roman emperor Caligula once declared war on Neptune, the god of the sea. He ordered his soldiers to march to the shore and attack the ocean by stabbing the waves with their swords. Afterward, he had them collect seashells as spoils of war.

Napoleon Was Attacked by Bunnies

After signing the Treaties of Tilsit in 1807, Napoleon Bonaparte decided to celebrate by organizing a rabbit hunt. His men rounded up hundreds of rabbits, but instead of fleeing, the rabbits attacked Napoleon and his party. The emperor fled in his carriage, unable to stop the relentless bunny assault.

The Great Emu War

In 1932, Australia faced an unusual foe—emus. The flightless birds were destroying crops in Western Australia, so the government sent soldiers equipped with machine guns to deal with them. However, the emus proved too agile, and after several attempts, the soldiers retreated. The emus won the "war," and the farmers were left to deal with the birds on their own.

The Time Julius Caesar
Was Kidnapped by Pirates

Before becoming Rome's most famous leader, Julius Caesar was kidnapped by pirates. When they demanded a ransom, Caesar laughed and told them they should ask for more. He even befriended the pirates and spent his time with them joking and reciting poetry. However, after being released, Caesar returned with his army, captured the pirates, and had them all executed.

The Dancing Plague of 1518

In the summer of 1518, the people of Strasbourg, France, were struck by a mysterious condition where they couldn't stop dancing. Dozens of people danced uncontrollably for days, and many collapsed from exhaustion. The cause remains unclear, but the bizarre "dancing plague" is well documented in historical records.

The Eiffel Tower Was Almost a Giant Guillotine

When the Eiffel Tower was being built for the 1889 World's Fair in Paris, it was initially met with opposition. Some critics suggested it would be better as a giant guillotine to represent France's revolutionary past. Fortunately, the idea didn't catch on, and the Eiffel Tower became a beloved symbol of France.

Benjamin Franklin's Air Bath Routine

Founding father Benjamin Franklin was known for his eccentric habits, including his "air baths." He believed that fresh air was essential to good health, so he would sit naked in front of an open window for about an hour each day, claiming it kept him clean and refreshed.

George Washington's Presidential Dental Woes

It's no secret that George Washington had dental problems, but the details are quite amusing. Contrary to popular belief, his dentures were not made of wood. They were crafted from a mix of materials, including human teeth, animal teeth, and even hippopotamus ivory. He struggled with his ill-fitting dentures throughout his presidency.

Queen Victoria Loved Cocaine

In the 19th century, cocaine was not only legal but considered a miracle cure. Queen Victoria herself was known to use a tincture of cocaine for her headaches, and she even gifted it to her friends. It wasn't until years later that the dangerous effects of the drug were recognized.

The Trial of a Pig

In medieval Europe, it wasn't uncommon for animals to be put on trial for crimes. In 1386, a sow was accused of killing a child and was put on trial in France. The pig was found guilty and executed in a public ceremony, dressed in human clothes for the occasion.

The Time the Pope Put a Dead Man on Trial

In one of the strangest episodes in papal history, Pope Stephen VI held the "Cadaver Synod" in 897, where he put the corpse of his predecessor, Pope Formosus, on trial. The body was exhumed, dressed in papal robes, and propped up in court to face accusations of violating church laws. Unsurprisingly, the dead pope was found guilty.

Tycho Brahe's Golden Nose

The famous Danish astronomer Tycho Brahe lost part of his nose in a duel over a math problem. He wore a prosthetic nose made of gold and silver for the rest of his life. It's said that he kept different noses for different occasions, making him a historical trendsetter in prosthetics.

Einstein's Pickle Obsession

Albert Einstein, one of the greatest minds in history, had some quirky habits. He was reportedly obsessed with pickles and ate them with nearly every meal. He even kept jars of pickles in his office for snacking while he worked on his scientific theories.

The Prank War Between Edison and Tesla

The rivalry between Thomas Edison and Nikola Tesla was legendary, but it also had its share of pranks. Edison would publicly mock Tesla's ideas, and Tesla once electrocuted a metal chair in Edison's lab to give him a nasty surprise. Their feud was both a battle of inventions and a game of one-upmanship.

The Boston Molasses Disaster

In 1919, a storage tank containing over 2 million gallons of molasses exploded in Boston, sending a massive wave of sticky syrup flooding through the streets. The molasses wave was so powerful that it knocked over buildings and killed 21 people. It took months to clean up the mess.

The Chicken That Lived Without a Head

In 1945, a farmer in Colorado accidentally cut off the head of a chicken named Mike, but to his surprise, the chicken didn't die. Mike lived for 18 months without a head, fed through an eyedropper, and became a sideshow attraction known as "Mike the Headless Chicken."

The Mystery of the Exploding Pants

In the 1930s, New Zealand farmers began using a chemical spray to kill weeds in their fields. Unfortunately, the chemical reacted with the fabric of their pants, causing some farmers' trousers to catch fire or explode. The phenomenon became known as the "exploding pants epidemic."

The Woman Who Sued the Devil

In 1971, a woman named Gerald Mayo filed a lawsuit in Pennsylvania against Satan. She claimed that the devil had caused her life to be filled with misery and accused him of being responsible for all her misfortunes. The court dismissed the case, ruling that they had no jurisdiction over Satan.

The War of the Stray Dog

In 1925, a stray dog crossing the border between Greece and Bulgaria caused an international incident. A Greek soldier chased the dog into Bulgarian territory, which led to a skirmish between the two countries. The "War of the Stray Dog" lasted only a few days but resulted in several casualties before the situation was resolved.

Day 20: Funny Fails:
When Science Went Wrong

Science has brought us incredible inventions, medical advancements, and life-changing discoveries, but not every experiment goes according to plan. Throughout history, there have been some hilarious, bizarre, and downright disastrous scientific fails. Here are some of the funniest moments when science didn't quite hit the mark:

The Exploding Whale

In 1970, authorities in Florence, Oregon, were faced with the problem of a dead sperm whale that had washed up on shore. Their solution? Blow it up with dynamite. Unfortunately, the explosion sent massive chunks of whale blubber flying into the air, some landing on cars over a quarter of a mile away. The "exploding whale" incident became legendary for its absurdity and was definitely not the clean-up solution they had hoped for.

The Swedish Warship
That Sank Immediately

In 1628, Sweden launched the Vasa, a massive warship meant to be the pride of the Swedish navy. Unfortunately, the ship was too top-heavy, and on its maiden voyage, it tipped over and sank just minutes after leaving the harbor. The Vasa lay on the sea floor for over 300 years before being recovered, and today, it stands as a museum piece —a reminder of poor design choices.

The Great London Beer Flood

In 1814, a massive vat of beer at the Meux and Company Brewery in London exploded, sending 1.4 million liters of beer rushing through the streets. The flood destroyed homes and killed eight people, drowning them in beer. It was a tragic yet bizarre disaster that has gone down in history as one of the strangest industrial accidents.

Nuclear Submarines Powered by Bananas

In 1965, the U.S. Navy mistakenly thought that bananas could emit radiation due to their potassium content. In an attempt to detect radiation, a nuclear submarine crew began testing bananas on board. They eventually realized that bananas weren't the radioactive threat they thought, and the experiment was quickly abandoned.

The Rocket-Powered Car That Crashed

In the 1970s, a group of rocket enthusiasts in the U.S. attempted to create a rocket-powered car, hoping to break speed records. However, the car's rocket misfired, causing the vehicle to crash and disintegrate in a fiery explosion. The stuntman driving the car survived, but the crash remains one of the most spectacular—and failed—rocket experiments in automotive history.

The Bird That Shut Down the Large Hadron Collider

In 2009, a piece of bread dropped by a bird caused the Large Hadron Collider—the world's largest particle accelerator—to overheat and shut down. The bird dropped the bread onto an electrical substation, leading to an electrical fault that temporarily halted operations. Even the most advanced technology can be brought to its knees by something as simple as a bird's snack!

The Tangled-Up Escape Balloon

During World War II, Nazi Germany tried to develop an escape balloon that could help pilots stranded at sea. However, during tests, the balloon's long, tangled ropes kept snagging on everything from trees to buildings, making it practically useless. The project was quietly abandoned, leaving the bizarre contraption as a testament to failed military innovation.

The Collapsing Tacoma Narrows Bridge

In 1940, the Tacoma Narrows Bridge in Washington state became famous for collapsing in dramatic fashion just four months after it opened. The bridge's design flaws caused it to twist violently in the wind, leading to its eventual destruction. The footage of the collapsing bridge, nicknamed "Galloping Gertie," became iconic, showing how nature can easily defeat even our most ambitious constructions.

The Time NASA Lost a Spacecraft Due to a Math Error

In 1999, NASA's $125 million Mars Climate Orbiter crashed into Mars because engineers had failed to convert English units to metric units. The spacecraft entered the Martian atmosphere at the wrong angle and disintegrated. It was a costly reminder that even the smallest mistakes can lead to disastrous consequences in space exploration.

The Hair-Growing Machine That Didn't Work

In the 1920s, a doctor named Albert C. Geyser invented a machine that he claimed could stimulate hair growth by shooting mild radiation at the scalp. Thousands of people tried the machine in the hope of regrowing their hair, but it soon became clear that not only did it not work, but it could also cause serious health problems. The device was quickly taken off the market.

The Chocolate-covered Cows Experiment

In the 1930s, a group of scientists thought it would be a good idea to coat cows in chocolate to protect them from the sun. They hoped that the chocolate would act as a protective layer and keep the cows cool. However, the cows hated being covered in chocolate, and the experiment ended in failure—and probably some very sticky cows.

The Mouse Utopia
That Went Horribly Wrong

In the 1960s, a scientist named John B. Calhoun conducted an experiment to create a "mouse utopia," where mice had everything they needed: food, shelter, and plenty of space. Initially, the mouse population thrived, but over time, the mice became aggressive, stopped reproducing, and eventually the colony collapsed. The experiment showed that even in ideal conditions, overcrowding can lead to societal collapse.

The 19th Century Balloon Mail Fail

During the Franco-Prussian War, the French government attempted to use hot air balloons to send mail over enemy lines. However, many of the balloons went off course, with some drifting into enemy territory and others landing as far away as Norway. Needless to say, the experiment wasn't the most effective way to deliver letters.

The Railway That Ate Its Passengers

In the 1800s, one of the earliest steam trains, the Adelaide, had an unusual flaw. The design of its engine created so much smoke and soot that passengers sitting near the front of the train would leave covered in grime, as if they had been "eaten" by the train. It was a literal example of a design gone wrong.

The Smelly Space Experiment

In 2008, scientists tried to recreate the scent of outer space for astronauts training on Earth. They found that space has a metallic smell, similar to hot metal or welding fumes. However, when the scent was synthesized for training purposes, it was so unpleasant that astronauts refused to wear their space suits during the trials, causing the experiment to be scrapped.

The Failed Flea Bombs

In World War II, Japanese scientists attempted to develop "flea bombs" that would spread diseases like plague through fleas dropped on enemy populations. The bombs were unreliable, and many exploded in the wrong areas or failed to spread disease effectively. Thankfully, the weapon was never fully deployed.

The Whale Carcass
That Stank Up an Entire Town

In 1999, the Taiwanese government decided to move a massive, decomposing whale carcass through the streets of Tainan. During transportation, the whale exploded due to built-up gases, covering the town in whale guts and causing a stench that lasted for days. It was a smelly disaster that residents will never forget.

The Bulletproof Glass Test Fail

In 1931, an inventor was trying to demonstrate the strength of his new bulletproof glass by shooting at it in front of an audience. Unfortunately, the glass shattered, and the bullet narrowly missed the inventor. Luckily, no one was injured, but the demonstration was far from a success.

The Pigeon-Guided Missile

During World War II, the U.S. military tried to develop a missile guided by pigeons. The idea was to train pigeons to peck at a target, and their movements would direct the missile. Though the concept was actually feasible, it was ultimately scrapped for more reliable forms of technology.

Day 21: Silly Superstitions: The Most Absurd Beliefs from Around the Globe

Superstitions have been a part of human culture for centuries, and while some seem reasonable, others are downright absurd. From lucky charms to strange rituals, these beliefs often defy logic but continue to be passed down through generations. Here are some of the silliest and most bizarre superstitions from around the world:

Whistling Indoors Brings Bad Luck (Russia)

In Russia, it's believed that whistling indoors will bring financial misfortune and drive away wealth. So, if you're in a Russian household, it's best to keep the whistling for outdoor activities!

Stepping in Dog Poop is Good Luck... Sometimes (France)

In France, stepping in dog poop with your left foot is considered good luck, while stepping in it with your right foot is seen as a bad omen. Either way, it's probably not a pleasant experience!

Sweeping Over Someone's Feet Dooms Them to Never Marry (Italy)

In Italy, there's a superstition that if you sweep over someone's feet with a broom, they'll never get married. This is a warning for anyone cleaning the floor—watch where you sweep!

The Curse of the Evil Eye (Mediterranean Region)

In countries around the Mediterranean, such as Greece and Turkey, the evil eye is believed to be a powerful curse caused by envious looks. People wear protective charms, often in the shape of blue eyes, to ward off this malevolent stare.

Hanging a Horseshoe Upside Down Will Bring Bad Luck (UK & USA)

Horseshoes are considered lucky charms in many cultures, but in the UK and USA, hanging one upside down is said to drain all its luck. It's believed that the good fortune will spill out and leave you empty-handed.

Knocking on Wood to Avoid Jinxing Yourself
(Various Countries)

The phrase "knock on wood" is used around the world to prevent bad luck after making a positive statement. For example, if someone says, "I've never been sick this year," they might knock on wood to avoid "jinxing" themselves.

Friday the 13th is Unlucky
(Western Cultures)

One of the most well-known superstitions is the fear of Friday the 13th, which is considered an unlucky day in many Western cultures. The origins of this belief are murky, but it continues to cause people to avoid making important decisions or flying on this ominous day.

Birds Flying Into Your House
is a Sign of Death (Various Cultures)

In several cultures, particularly in parts of Europe and North America, a bird flying into your house is seen as a bad omen, often symbolizing death. People believe it's a warning of misfortune to come, especially if it's a black bird.

Breaking a Mirror Brings Seven Years of Bad Luck (Western Cultures)

One of the oldest superstitions is that breaking a mirror will bring seven years of bad luck. This belief dates back to ancient times when people thought mirrors held a piece of the soul, and breaking one would damage it.

Don't Open an Umbrella Indoors (Various Cultures)

It's considered bad luck to open an umbrella indoors, with people fearing that it will bring misfortune or even physical harm. The superstition likely comes from the danger of handling large umbrellas indoors, where they could knock things over or cause accidents.

Don't Cut Your Nails at Night (India & Japan)

In both Indian and Japanese cultures, it's believed that cutting your nails at night will bring bad luck or even shorten your life. This superstition may have practical roots, as cutting nails in dim light could lead to injury.

Tucking Your Thumb When Passing a Graveyard (Japan)

In Japan, it's customary to tuck your thumbs into your fists when passing a graveyard. The word for "thumb" in Japanese means "parent," so tucking in your thumb is believed to protect your parents from death.

Walking Under a Ladder is Bad Luck (Western Cultures)

Walking under a ladder is another well-known superstition that's believed to bring bad luck. This belief might stem from the dangers of walking under a precarious object, but some say it has religious origins, as the triangle formed by a ladder leaning against a wall was seen as sacred.

Spilling Salt Brings Misfortune, Unless You Throw It Over Your Shoulder (Western Cultures)

Spilling salt is thought to bring bad luck in many Western cultures, but there's a way to avoid it: throw a pinch of the spilled salt over your left shoulder to ward off evil spirits. This superstition dates back to ancient times when salt was a valuable commodity.

Don't Gift a Knife—It Will Cut the Relationship (Various Cultures)

In many cultures, giving someone a knife as a gift is believed to sever the relationship between the giver and the recipient. To avoid this, some people give a coin along with the knife, which the recipient gives back as "payment," symbolically preventing the relationship from being cut.

Crossing Paths with a Black Cat Brings Bad Luck (Western Cultures)

Black cats have long been associated with witches and bad luck, and in many Western cultures, crossing paths with one is thought to bring misfortune. However, in some places, black cats are seen as symbols of good luck!

Wishing on a Fallen Eyelash (Various Cultures)

If you find a fallen eyelash on your cheek, make a wish and blow it away for good luck. This charming superstition is common in various cultures and is believed to grant wishes or bring luck.

Day 22. Wild Weather Wonders: Nature's Extreme Moments

Get ready to dive into some of the wildest, most jaw-dropping weather phenomena Mother Nature has up her sleeve! These extreme events are nature's way of showing off – sometimes beautiful, sometimes terrifying, and sometimes so strange it's hard to believe they're real. Here are a few of nature's most fascinating weather wonders:

Raining Fish and Frogs

It sounds unbelievable, but in certain places, it really does rain... fish and frogs! How? Powerful storms and tornadoes sometimes lift small creatures from water sources and carry them over great distances, eventually dropping them in completely different locations. In Honduras, there's even a yearly "Fish Rain" that's become legendary!

Thundersnow: Lightning in a Snowstorm

Snowstorms are rare enough, but when lightning strikes during a blizzard, you get "thundersnow"! Instead of rain, lightning appears in the middle of heavy snow, creating an eerie yet amazing light show in the snowflakes. Thundersnow is especially rare, occurring mainly in super cold regions.

Ball Lightning: Floating Fireballs

One of the most mysterious weather events, ball lightning looks like a glowing orb that hovers in the air, moving slowly before it vanishes as suddenly as it appeared. Scientists are still working to understand it, but one thing's for sure – it's both fascinating and a little spooky!

Haboob: The Massive Wall of Dust

Haboobs are intense dust storms that form in dry regions like the deserts of Africa and the Middle East. They're massive enough to blot out the sky and turn day into night. This enormous wall of dust rushes forward with incredible speed – an awe-inspiring, yet terrifying sight.

Ice Tsunami: The Frozen Wave

When lake ice begins to thaw and strong winds kick in, huge sheets of ice can be pushed onto land, creating an "ice tsunami." These icy waves can move across the ground, damaging buildings in their path. In 2013, an ice tsunami in Minnesota saw waves reaching over 30 feet high!

Blood Rain: The Eerie Red Downpour

"Blood rain" happens when rain takes on a reddish tint, thanks to dust or algae particles carried in the atmosphere. This creepy-looking phenomenon has been observed in India and Spain, among other places – and while it may look supernatural, there's nothing magical about it!

Each of these phenomena is a reminder of nature's unpredictability and sheer power. The natural world is always surprising us – sometimes dazzling, sometimes scary, but always inspiring a sense of wonder at the forces that shape our planet.

Day 23. Tricky Trivia: Test Your Knowledge!

Ready to put your knowledge to the test? Here's a set of fun, tricky trivia questions to see how much you've picked up! Try not to scroll to the answers until you're ready – some of these might catch you off guard!

1. Which animal has the most taste buds?
a) Dogs b) Humans c) Catfish d) Parrots

2. What's the only letter that doesn't appear in any U.S. state name?
a) Q b) Z c) X d) J

3. How long can a snail sleep?
a) 3 days b) 3 weeks c) 3 months d) 3 years

4. Which planet has the most moons?
a) Earth b) Jupiter c) Saturn d) Mars

5. Which country eats the most chocolate per capita?
a) USA b) Switzerland c) Japan d) Brazil

6. What's the rarest M&M color?
a) Red b) Brown c) Blue d) Green

7. Which city is known as the "City of a Thousand Minarets"?
a) Istanbul b) Cairo c) Dubai d) Marrakech

8. True or False: Bananas grow on trees.

9. How much of the Earth's surface is covered in water?
a) 50% b) 60% c) 70% d) 80%

10. Which country has the most time zones?
a) USA b) Russia c) China d) France

Answers:
c) Catfish
a) Q
d) 3 years
c) Saturn
b) Switzerland
b) Brown
b) Cairo
False
c) 70%
d) France

Day 24: Christmas Curiosities: Fun and Unbelievable Holiday Facts

As a book destined for a holiday stocking, it's only fitting to end with some delightful and unexpected facts about the most wonderful time of the year—Christmas! From bizarre traditions to surprising holiday records, here are some fun and unbelievable facts about Christmas that will surely put you in the festive spirit:

The World's Largest Christmas Stocking

The largest Christmas stocking ever made measured over 168 feet long and 70 feet wide. Created in Italy in 2011, it was big enough to hold more than 1,000 presents!

Jingle Bells Wasn't Originally a Christmas Song

Believe it or not, "Jingle Bells" was originally written for Thanksgiving, not Christmas! Composed in 1857, it became one of the most popular Christmas songs, despite its original purpose.

The Origins of Candy Canes
Candy canes were first created in the 17th century in Germany, and they weren't even peppermint flavored. Originally white and straight, they were bent into a cane shape to represent a shepherd's staff, symbolizing the shepherds who visited baby Jesus.

Japan's KFC Christmas Tradition
In Japan, it's a Christmas tradition to eat KFC! Thanks to a clever marketing campaign in the 1970s, millions of Japanese families now celebrate the holiday by ordering a bucket of fried chicken from Kentucky Fried Chicken.

The Tallest Christmas Tree Ever
The tallest Christmas tree on record was a staggering 221 feet tall, displayed in a Washington mall in 1950. That's about the height of a 20-story building!

Spider Webs as Christmas Decorations
In Ukraine, it's considered good luck to decorate your tree with spider webs! According to legend, a poor widow couldn't afford ornaments for her Christmas tree, so spiders spun webs to decorate it for her. To this day, Ukrainians hang artificial spider webs for good fortune.

The Christmas Truce of 1914

During World War I, on Christmas Eve 1914, British and German soldiers called an unofficial truce, left their trenches, and celebrated together. They exchanged gifts, sang carols, and even played soccer in a remarkable moment of holiday peace during the war.

Santa Claus Wears Red Because of Coca-Cola

While Santa Claus has been depicted in various colors over the centuries, his modern red suit became iconic in the 1930s thanks to Coca-Cola's advertising campaigns. The company's holiday ads cemented the jolly figure in red as the Santa we know today.

World's Largest Snowman

The world's largest snowman, built in 2008 in Maine, USA, stood 122 feet tall and was named Olympia after the state senator. She even had tree trunks for arms and eyelashes made of skis!

The Tradition of Christmas Pickles

A quirky Christmas tradition in some parts of the world involves hiding a glass pickle ornament deep within the branches of the Christmas tree. The first person to find the pickle on Christmas morning is said to receive good luck or an extra present!

The Real 12 Days of Christmas
The 12 days of Christmas aren't the 12 days leading up to Christmas but the days following, starting on December 25 and ending on January 6 with the Feast of the Epiphany.

Christmas Lights Were Invented by Edison
Thomas Edison, the famous inventor, is credited with creating the first strand of Christmas lights in 1880. He strung lights around his laboratory and later marketed them as a safer alternative to candles on Christmas trees.

World's Largest Secret Santa Gift Exchange
In 2013, Reddit users organized the world's largest Secret Santa gift exchange, with more than 85,000 people from 160 countries participating. Gifts ranged from small tokens to elaborate, personalized presents.

The Fastest Time to Decorate a Christmas Tree
The record for the fastest time to decorate a Christmas tree is an impressive 34.52 seconds, set by Sharon Juantuah from the UK in 2018. Talk about speedy holiday spirit!

Printed in Great Britain
by Amazon

50102766R00057